T0380651

Soft, Inspiring Reflections on Essential Oils

Yvonne M. Boudreau, MDiv

Foreword by Christopher J. Fabricius, ND
Founder of Living Medicine

To order additional copies of this book, contact:
Xlibris
844-714-8691
www.Xlibris.com
Orders@Xlibris.com

ISBN: 978-1-6641-6657-8 (sc)
ISBN: 978-1-6641-6658-5 (hc)
ISBN: 978-1-6641-6656-1 (e)

Library of Congress Control Number: 2021906825

Print information available on the last page

Rev. date: 04/22/2021

Dedication

To my sister, Louise, who first introduced me to Young Living Essential Oils many years ago.

And to Michelle, my companion and friend on the journey, who is a true partner in crime when it comes to exploring and experimenting with new and old oils. Whatever oil we are going to indulge in always ends up being the perfect adventure and experience.

I love you both.

Contents

Foreword

As a practicing primary care and naturopathic physician, I hold a broad and wholistic perspective on human nature. The following words express what I believe to be true about essential oils. It is my sincerest hope that this foreword will set the stage and the tone for the beautiful reflections contained in the following pages.

Ancient wisdom, philosophies, and religions from multiple native cultures around the world speak to the complex, multidimensional, divine nature that is inherent within each of us as human beings. In the simplest of terms, human beings are composed of physical, mental, emotional, and spiritual aspects. Any physicist will tell you that what we perceive as being solid material with five senses is actually 99.99 percent energy, with only a tiny portion being actual material. Hence, it is one's Spirit that animates and imbues our bodies with life.

Classical Chinese medical philosophy tells us that in human beings, Spirit (referred to as Shen) is carried within the blood and housed within the heart. Through our blood, this Spirit is conveyed throughout the physical, emotional, mental, and spiritual levels of our being, along with the essential information and energy it carries and conveys.

The same principle is true in plant life. The Spirit of each plant is carried within the essential oils of the plant. Therefore, the essential oils of a plant convey more than simply the biochemical set of molecules that constitute its material form. They also convey the plant's sentience—its knowledge, memory, and experience.

I am always humbled and surprised to realize that from a chemical perspective, human hemoglobin and chlorophyll are not that dissimilar biochemically from plant life; in the end, we possess a close bond with plant life. We have much in common with plants as we are all constrained and buoyed by the same elemental forces and laws of nature.

Nowadays, a growing number of primary care physicians like myself know of, respect, and make use of the impressive biochemical, immune, hormone, and neurotransmitter modulatory benefits that are attributed to the material chemical makeup of essential oils to improve our patients' lives. However, in addition to these impressive physical/material biochemical benefits, there are also tremendous benefits that our bodies' emotional, mental, and spiritual levels derive from the energetic/informational transference that comes from using intact pure essential oils.

Such unmatched quality from Seed to Seal is what Young Living Essential Oils are renowned for and which I can personally attest to, having personally reviewed and inspected some of their distillation facilities and processes and having continuously employed them in my medical practice for more than two decades.

How we come to be who we are and what our intent was at the time of making the various decisions we all must make that ultimately dictate the course of our lives matters tremendously. Hence, the source of a work matters! It is my absolute honor to introduce to you the source of this beautiful work, Yvonne Boudreau, and to endorse the caliber of who she is.

I have known Yvonne for several years. I have had the privilege of seeing her gracefully navigate life challenges and painful experiences with poise, patience, presence, class, and humility, and all the while being a source of love to those around her. Her spirit is conveyed in this work and is sure to inspire yours!

This work you hold within your hands is truly a work of sincere joy, genuine love, and worthy insight. It is remarkable how eloquently Yvonne captures the spirit of each oil she has written an ode to! Its purpose is to catalyze your **own positive transformative journey and relationship with the essential oils you employ.**

You are in for a treat!

With Spirit,

Christopher J. Fabricius, ND
Founder of Living Medicine
www.LivingMedicine.com

Introduction

Several years ago, I began using Young Living Essential Oils on a regular basis. The more I used the oils, the more I began to reflect on the gift they had become in my life. Gradually, I realized that the plants, trees, bushes, flowers, and herbs that made up these oils were coming from the ground, from Mother Nature, into my being. Hence, I grasped a deeper and more spiritual connectivity to nature and my inner being.

Young Living Essential Oils have become a part of my spiritual journey. I derive great joy and pleasure from reflecting on the oils. From this place of quiet and solitude, I put pen to paper to give expression to what I was thinking, feeling, and experiencing as I continued to use these amazing, 100 percent therapeutic-grade oils.

My writing does not come from looking at the chemical compounds or the scientific properties that make up these oils. My writing comes from a more poetic/prose/reflective/prayer style of writing. I know these odes come from a place of contemplation. They come from my heart. They come from a divine source. They come from having lived life and being fortunate enough to have been open and receptive to each new chapter of my life.

I would never be audacious enough to call myself a poet. But if someone should think of these prose and reflections as poetry, then I can only feel humbled, knowing that I was certainly led and guided by a reality beyond me.

Finally, it is my hope and desire that you might find some inspiration, a glimmer of hope, an irresistible smile, a passageway to an important insight, or simply the joy of reading words that might connect you to your deeper self.

So may the gift of oils, the gift of Mother Nature, bring us to a Spirit-led life.

Harmony

Integrity,
  intuitive,
    instinctual.
To be in harmony is
  to be an open vessel,
  to be a maker of trust,
  to be a paver of humility,
  to be a practitioner of compassion,
  to be a creator of inner and outer sacred spaces,
  to be architects of dynamic becoming
    that is in harmony with nature, with others,
      with our own dynamic inner mystery.

Geranium

Ancient friend,
Exceptional healer,
Bringer of balance,
Source of comfort.

Holder of properties
    for regenerating skin and spirit.
Restorer of health,
    carrier of mental, spiritual, and emotional
       balance.
Geranium, I hold you as precious;
   beyond imagining
     is your amazing and sweet ability to uplift
       my soul.

Wintergreen

You sound like winter,
but no matter the season,
you are always calling from deep within.
Wintergreen,
you are always green-ing my spirit.
Green
growth
generosity
is your gift.
Wintergreen—
stabilizer,
sanctifier.
sanctuary for healing and soothing.

9

Melrose

You are a hidden gem.
   A humble oil,
      giver of comfort,
         everyday go-to rescuer.
Melrose,
   unassuming and mighty,
      source of protection from
         all scrapes, bruises, cuts, and wounds of life.

Dream Catcher

Dreams are the language of the night,
  of the unconscious speaking to me.

Dreams deserve my attention
  to untangle the messages I cannot hear in my awakened hours.

Dream Catcher, you help me remember the pieces of my night journey
  that I might give better direction to my daytime endeavors.

Dream Catcher, you never fail to open yet another gateway
  for me to fall ever deeper into the mystery and wonder of dreaming.

Three Wise Men

Three Wise Men?
Or is it Three Wise Women?
Or could it be Three Wise Angels?
No matter the name,
this precious oil brings
wisdom in abundance.
Source of ever-flowing love.
May this oil continue to
lead,
guide,
hold,
and
guard
me on the sacred journey.

Grounding

Grounding is allowing
my inner and outer being to align.

The cycle of receiving and giving,
   laughing and crying,
      engaging and retreating,
         outflowing and inflowing,
            acting and contemplating.

Keeping me in balance,
   keeping me grounded,
      keeping me firmly connected
         to Mother Earth.

Grounding always invites me
   to become solidly steeped
      in my inner source of strength and well-being.

When I am grounded there is no discernable space
   between the divine and my soul.

Sacred Mountain

Connecting earth and sky,
  connecting heart and soul,
    connecting human and divine.

Mountains invite us to look
  at life from different perspectives.

It is only on the sacred mountain
  that we can see the face of God and live.

Cedarwood

Oh, ancient friend,
how is it that I can feel
your roots deep in the earth?

Cedarwood: life-giving tree,
faithful, sturdy holder of
thousands of years of secrets.

What a holy moment to
hold and feel your essence
in the pouring out of
your life energy for my well-being.

Valor

Valor, you always make me feel ready for the day ahead.

My day begins with the power of Valor applied to the bottom of
my feet, then my wrists, and onto my sacrum.

Each day my body awaits the ritual of Valor seeping to my bloodstream,
giving courage and strength
to my day,
to my soul,
to my spirit.

Myrtle

How is it that you can be contained in a little bottle?

You are a powerhouse of wellness.

Shrub of beauty,

Promise of goodness,

Ever-greening plant of fragrant delight.

Touching cells and molecules, altering, shifting.

Maker of rightness and bringer of gladness.

Arriving on the gentle breeze of love made visible.

Higher Unity

Depth of Oneness,
Perfect pitch,
Unified sound,
Silent harmony.

Highest chakra,
Journey to infinity,
Beyond knowing,
Eye of the sacred.

Grace-giver,
Companion in the darkness,
Soundless vibrations,
Convergence of visible and invisible mystery.

Marjoram

Oh, spice of life!
Relaxer of muscles,
scent of delight,
melter of tension.

Marjoram, I pour you generously
on my aching places.
I cannot count the times you have saved
the night because of leg cramps.

So, I treasure and value
your ancient place
of prominence in all herbal cabinets.

Ravintsara

Powerhouse of healing properties.

My inhalations of Ravintsara bring sweet
surrender of unwanted burdens.

My exhalations of Ravintsara bring quiet
gratitude for the lavish gift of openness.

Ravintsara, you are
My faithful friend on all journeys.
Purifier of air,
supporter of breath.

Ravintsara, you reach into the inner chambers
of my being,
bringing solace,
relief,
and unsurpassed delight.

Field

Creator of energy fields I cannot see.

This oil helps me bring into being
   positive thoughts and
      feelings of new possibilities.

Field helps generate
   attitudes that enhance
      balance,
         confidence,
            courage.

Field expands what is inconceivable
   and makes it imaginable.
      Potential becomes reality.

Field assures me that there are always options.

As I invite more positive energy,
   my field of attracting
      more life-giving energy
         grows wider, deeper, broader
            into fields and spaces
that are inward and outward flowing catalysts
      for living life to the fullest.

Fun

Okay,
Fun is fun!

We are created
To laugh,
To be silly,
To enjoy,
To be happy,
To dance,
To play,
To relax.

Oh,
And did you notice
All this happens
When we are
In relationship
And
In community?

Fun is the oil that
Brings me balance—
God knows I take life way too seriously.
Fun
Makes me smile.
Reminds me
To look deep
Within
For joy.

Clarity

Sometimes we need
  the fog,
    the dark,
      the chaos,
        and the confusion.

Sometimes we need
  to explore the hidden terrain,
    to experience the deepest of night,
      to wander into the unknown,
        to embrace sorrow and grief.

Sometimes we only need
  to sit with mystery,
    to gaze upon our situation,
and then
  to simply,
    to lovingly,
      to compassionately,
        to openly
          ask for clarity.

Rose

Oil of my heart,

Highest of frequencies,

Molecular healer,

Royal beauty of silent wonder,

Majestic power of love,

Enabler of dreams.

Rose, gift from beyond our
galactic imaginings,
You open us to relationships that are
Respectful,
Honoring human dignity,
Reverent,
Authentic love.

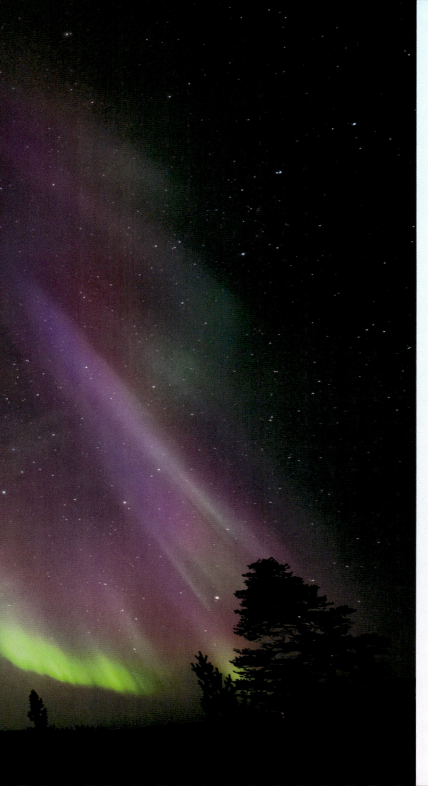

Northern Lights Black Spruce

We belong to light.
We belong to a true north.

Can you hear the blessed assurance
of being in nature's embrace?

Can you feel rooted
and grounded in an everlasting encirclement?

Can you smell the deep forest of evergreen
spilling into your bloodstream?

Can you taste the air that is alive
and wants to feed us
at the banquet of love?

33

Into the Future

We belong to evolution.

How strange that we would
seek and long for permanence
when we were born
in primordial fluidity.

We are destined
for the future;
we are evolving in
an ever-expanding universe.

We are always falling into
complexities that are
catapulting us into
no fixed place
in a universe,
into the future
filled with
unfolding mystery.

Beware cosmic
journey-maker.
Caution must be
surrendered.

Cypress

Tree of regal beauty
  and quiet strength.

Tree that inspires
  and invites transformation.

Tree of gentle pride
  always honoring the sacred.

Tree of reverence,
  giving perspective to
      our place in the universe.

Cypress,
  the green of serenity,
  the promoter of stability,
  the giver of hope.

Frankincense

Oil of Lebanon,
   Oil of anointing,
      Oil more precious than gold.

Oil of hidden powers
  To heal,
     To calm,
       To restore.

Oil given to us by the divine,
  Bridge to the sacred.

Highest expression of all things holy.

Frankincense, you are wisdom,
  you are transcendence,
    you are transformation,
     you are adaptation,
       you are the gift sublime!

Abundance

Source of all that is.

You who are Abundance itself,
always calling us to
receive life in abundance.

Truly, my blessings on this earthy journey are
   pressed down
     and overflowing
with the abundance of life, peace, and abiding love.

Joy

If Joy is about being
  in quiet serenity,
    in amazement,
      in peaceful openness,
        then I feel joy.

If Joy is about being
  in awe,
    in wonderment,
      in contentment,
        then I feel joy.

If Joy is about being
  wrapped in compassion
    and held by the presence of mystery,
      then I feel joy.

Inner Child

Sweet and gentle,
Raging and lashing.

Inner child,
Always evolving.
Even as an adult,
We return to the child,
Or
Is it the child that returns to me
In my wisdom years?

Inner child—
Holder
And
Possessor
Of your own wisdom.

Teach me that which
I forgot to
Be
For you,
O child of amazing grace.

White Angelica

Celestial wonder,
 Sublime inspiration.
   Subtle scent of
    Purest,
      Peace-filled,
       Perfectly
        Protecting essence.

Lavender

Wonder of nature,
  purple majesty,
    field of magic.

Harvested, processed, distilled,
  always giving,
    pouring goodness and gratitude.

Every season I call on Lavender.
  She is in my face,
    subtle,
      lasting,
        profound.
  She is energy on my:
skin,
soul,
heart,
mind,
entire being.

Lavender, you are the queen of wonderment.

Orange

Yellow glow,
　Refreshing smell,
　　Uplifting spirit.

Opening my mind
　To newness,
　　To change,
　　　To embracing
　　　　The now and the not yet.

Freedom

Oh, such a powerful word that can be—
Slippery,
  Slick,
    Solemn,
      Shifting,
        True, and even devious.

It's something that everyone wants.
Is it freedom to?
  Freedom from?
    Freedom with?
Is it up to the individual?
  Is there a community responsibility?
When I use the oil called Freedom and take it into myself,
  I feel freedom
    To love,
      To surrender,
        To embrace,
       To yield,
        To give.
I feel a freedom
  From materialism,
    From selfish tendencies,
      From myopic views,
        From my own self-interest.
I feel freedom
  Is being open to others,
    Is welcoming diversity,
      Is making room for community.

It's about being my best self
  And leaving a wide berth for others.

Egyptian Gold

Holy oil of ancient times,
I receive with deep gratitude
The richness of this oil.

I consciously and lovingly
Apply this oil, knowing
It will protect and guide me.

I can feel its lusciousness on my skin
As it seeps into my being.

I know that in the waiting
This oil will bring
The gifts my soul needs and desires.

Gentle Baby

To stand upright in life
Physically, mentally, emotionally, and
spiritually,
I require
  Human touch,
      Human interaction,
          Human intimacy.

Gentle Baby keeps me
  Soft,
      Tender,
          Supple,
              Malleable.

Gentle Baby brings me
  Home to myself when I have been
      Armored,
          Tense,
              Unrelenting,
                  Inconsiderate.

Gentle Baby returns me to my
  Truer,
      Gentler,
          Responsive self.

Peace and Calming

Peace and Calming?
Is there such a thing in nature
That can establish such a gigantic task
As giving peace and calming?

Mother Nature is a generous
Giver and healer.

She is generative in her wisdom.

To inhale the scent of Peace and Calming
Is to immediately remind the body
To breathe deeply.

To let the aroma settle
Into the nervous system.

And be willing
To let go,
To surrender,
To be in a state of calm and peace
With myself.

Peace and Calming, you are food for my soul
and the journey.

Dragon Time

Deep in the inner cave of my heart
　Rests a
　　　Timeless,
　　　　　Timely,
Mighty,
　Magical,
　　　Mythical,
　　　　Real,
　　　　　　Present power.

Mystical dragon,
　Eyes filled with courage,
　　　Heart open to dreams,
　　　　Ears acutely attuned to whispered hope.

Dragon Time,
　Quantum time traveler,
　　　Generous giver of strength,
　　　　Always present when I don't have
　　　　　Enough courage,
　　　　　　Enough dreams,
　　　　　　　Enough hope.

Christmas Spirit

Quiet joy.
Solid transcendence.
Anchor of contentment.
Beyond earthly seasons.
Herculean in strength.
Subtle presence.

M-Grain

Migraine,
  Headache,
    Heartache,
      Broken time,
        Arresting flow.

M-Grain,
Oil of hope,
Drench my spirt with your

  Soothing,

  Healing,

Surrendering spirit.

    Help me relax into

  Your liquid, rich oil seeping

Into every crevice and nook of

My headache and heartache.

Stress Away

Every inhalation brings
   A surprise,
   A pleasant reminder to relax,
   A willingness to be open,
   An awakened instinct to smile,
   A refreshing embrace,
   A delightful knowing that I am alive and loved.

Trauma Life

A fall.
A sudden unexpected twist in a relationship.
The unimaginable separation from a loved one.
The shock of sudden death.
An accident.
An assault—physical, mental, or emotional.

You know the trauma of life intimately.

Trauma Life eases the blunt reality.
Trauma Life brings a gentler ebb and flow to
Anger,
Sorrow,
Grief.

It is in the pain, in the trauma,
In the dark of night
That we wait and
Wait and
Wait
For the next unfolding.

Thieves

Thieves come in the night.

Little did they know their thievery
Would bring such wonderous
Knowledge against
  Plague, pandemic, virus, germs,
And enhance our ability
To purify our home environments.

I tip my hat to the delights of
thievery!

Myrrh

Gold, Frankincense, and Myrrh—
  Gifts to a newborn king.

Biblical Myrrh contains
  Many medicinal properties.

Myrrh comes to us from a thorny tree
  Oozing reddish-brown sap,
    Which yields to a rich, earthy, vacuous oil.

Myrrh, consecrated incense
  Used in worship and anointing.

The warmth of Myrrh is grounding
And promises well-being.

Myrrh, my friend in times of fatigue
And supporting my immune system.

Gathering

How easily I become
Scattered,
Cluttered,
Twisted,
Knotted,
Lost.

Gathering brings me
To my center,
To my inner strength,
To my better self,
To a deep knowing that
I belong to solidity,
I belong to holiness,
I belong to divine presence.

Gathering always
Steeps me in the reality
That my life is rich
With meaning,
With blessings,
With
Reverberating
Soundless
Grace.

German Chamomile

Pool of blue serenity,
Center of heart energy,
Dove of peace,
Fire of inner wisdom.

German Chamomile,
Blue ocean of gentle presence.
Calming breeze that eases
the disquieted mind and spirit.

Flower of soul essence,
Intuitive healer,
Resonance,
And
Bridge
To
The ever-present Comforter.

Believe

Intimate knower of
  Unseen energy fields.

Creator and sustainer
  Of an invisible force
    That is filled with unseen light.

Electromagnetic life
  And substantial reality.

Believe,
  Trust,
    Readiness,
      Higher consciousness,
        Bold sustainer of body, mind, and
        soul.

Entranceway to all the
  Beauty that surrounds us
    And is in us.

Forgiveness

Oil of Forgiveness,
So fragrant,
So smooth,
So inviting.

Forgiveness,
Such a difficult act for humans.

Yet not to forgive
Is costly beyond measure.

Forgiveness and time are
Inseparable partners.
Time to forgive self and others.
Time to surrender
Anger,
Resentment,
Hurts,
Deep wounds.
To forgive the unforgiveable.

Forgiveness
Requires non-clock-time reflection,
Inner spaciousness,
Quiet humbleness,
Openness,
Nondefensive posture,
Heart knowing that forgiveness is about love.

Oil of Forgiveness,
Bathe me in your sweet aroma
That melts that which
Is stubborn and unyielding in me.

Inspiration

What inspires you?
  What engenders inspiration
    In the human heart?

In our evolutionary cosmic world,
  I feel awe and wonderment
    By looking at creation.
      Because creation
        Is the visible
          Expression of the Creator.

A gentle breeze, the breath of God!

Matter is energy.
  Our universe is wild,
    Unpredictable,
      Unruly.
        Yet there is stability
          And direction.

Life gives way to love.

Inspiration is nurtured
  By absorbing
    Our interconnectedness,
    Our dynamic becoming,
    Our humble knowing that
      Our galaxy is one of millions of galaxies.

To hold and take in the oil of Inspiration
  Is to sink into humble mystery.

Envision

Awake, aware, and envisioning
  Angels of truth.

Free-flowing life force.

Envision your wise guides.

Give permission to
  That which cannot be changed.

Allow perspectives and horizons
  To broaden beyond the self.

Welcome new insights;
  Put on new lenses,
And focus on what
  You see with the eyes of your heart.

Use the eyes that can see in the dark.

Exercise the eyes that envision vital
energy
  Swirling in and around and beyond
    Your energetic space.

Raven

Raven oil,
   Intense,
      Penetrating,
         Focusing,
           Intriguing.

Raven oil,
   Like your sky-soaring friend raven,
   You have razor-sharp sight:
         Intuitive,
      Adaptable,
     Resolving issues,
   Confident.

Raven oil,
   Bringer of openness,
     Soother of discomfort,
       Balm of wellness,
         Enabler of deep breathing,
           Faithful friend and companion.

Rosemary

Light and bright,
Airy,
Seductive,
Addictive.

You possess culinary delights,
But I prefer your
Easing,
Melting,
Soothing,
Aromatic vigor,
Deeply healing,
And
Gently awakening abilities.

Rosemary,
You satisfy
The tendrils of my endless needs
For
Holy calm.

You strengthen
Memory
And
Generously
Give
Wit and Wisdom.

Basil

Gardener's friend.
Refreshing taste for the summer palate,
Gastronomical delight,
Scent of absolute bliss.

Basil and Tangerine intermingled
And defused
Create an
Atmosphere that
The senses
Long for over and over again.

Basil oil, you hold
A prized place in all
Ancient apothecary shelves.
Called on for
Body, mind, and spirit.

Holy, royal Basil,
You bring
Centeredness,
Balance,
Calm,
Clarity,
And
Fortify my being.

The following three pieces are simply other reflections on the oils in general.

The Sacred Oil Jar

These oils come into my life as pure gifts.
   Sometimes I think they are mine.
Sometimes I don't know if I want
the oils to seep
out of the jar and lavish
their healing properties upon me;
or
if I want to leap into the jar and be
   totally emersed in their
      lush,
         slick,
            slippery,
               supple goodness.
O giver of healing oils,
   you open yet another doorway
   that brings me always deeper
   into the mystery of you blessing my life.

Nourished

I am nourished by oils that come into my being
  in ways yet unknown to me.

Precious oils, heal those wounds that I don't even realize
  need tending and healing.

Those wounds seep and ooze toxins;
  they silently leak and sometimes spoil
    wells of clean, fresh water.

May these oils go to the very root
  of a wound,
    of a grudge,
      of a hurt,
        of a resentment
so that I can be free of that which hinders and debilitates.

May all oils from herbs, flowers, trees, bushes, and plants
  reunite me with the spirit of cosmic goodness.

The Treasury

I have a treasury,
yes, a treasury of oils.

Only my friend and I have access
to this treasury.

We dip into the treasury when the need arises.
That is, when someone is ill, in pain, has a discomfort,
or requires something for body, mind, or spirit.

It is a sacred treasury that is always being replenished.

It is good for my soul to know that many have been rescued by
Raven, RC, White Angelica, Marjoram, Lavender, Tea Tree, Purification.

It's more than an emergency medicine kit.
   It is a well of liquid gold,
        a holy alchemy,
             an apothecary for life
waiting to impart its essence for our healing, which is
ever-evolving and in dynamic becoming.

Printed in the United States
by Baker & Taylor Publisher Services